Stylish
CRAFT FOAM
✦PROJECTS✦

Easy-to-Make Wreaths, Party Décor, and More

Lisa Fulmer

D1737445

TABLE OF CONTENTS

Introduction 4   Tips and Techniques 8

Craft Foam Basics. 6   Materials 12

Woodland Wreath 14   Washi Tape Décor Balls. . . 16   Entwined Wreath 18

Sandy Beach Sign 20   Triple-Take Mirrors. 22   Candy Stripes Wreath 24

Country Cream Topiary. . . 26   Crystal Snowball
Garland. 28   Romance Triptych
Wall Panels 30

Pink Champagne Party
Garland 32

Beaded Burlap Tree 34

Atomic Mobile 36

Mini Layer Cake 38

Scented Pearl
Pomanders 40

Modern Monogram
Wall Panels 42

Cake Pop Cube 44

Blooming Block 46

Craft foam is the perfect starting point for making so many different kinds of fabulous projects—for any style, any budget, and any skill level.

For gifts, home décor, party trimming, and holiday crafts, craft foam is an ideal foundation. Not only is it inexpensive and easy to work with, it's also an incredibly versatile surface that unites well with many other creative materials. Paint, fabric, scrapbook paper, glitter, ribbons...all of your favorite craft supplies can be used with craft foam in more ways than you can imagine to bring one-of-a-kind ideas to life. Inside this book, you'll learn how to make a variety of stylish topiaries, wreaths, party garlands, and more. Even if you've never worked with craft foam before, you can achieve success with each and every one of these projects. Use what's in your stash or go out and get inspired by the newest products at your local craft store. This book is all about expressing your own DIY style—so whether you're entertaining guests, creating a gift, or looking to make an inviting wreath to welcome the family home for the holidays, we've got you covered.

Come on, let's have fun with foam!

Craft Foam Basics

The two most common brands of rigid, dimensional craft foam are Smoothfoam™ and Styrofoam™. Both brands make their product from polystyrene, but the manufacturing process is different for their sheets, balls, and other shapes. What crafters really need to know is how the difference in manufacturing impacts the surface. Smoothfoam (expanded foam or smooth foam) is smooth and dense, while Styrofoam (extruded foam or textured foam) is textured and crunchy. Both kinds of craft foam can be used interchangeably in many types of projects, but they do each have unique properties that sometimes lend themselves better to certain techniques.

Smooth foam is lovely to paint, distress, and heat-carve, and it hugs straight pins and wires tightly. Textured foam is great for dry floral arranging or when you need to easily poke in thicker items like chenille stems. The texture is also perfect when you want a crystallized effect. Both types of foam are inexpensive and very lightweight, making them ideal for centerpieces, garlands, and wall art. Once you get a feel for how each type works with different materials, let your imagination run wild!

Other types of foam commonly used in crafting (but not featured in this book) include:

- **Floral foam:** holds water for live flower arrangements
- **Craft foam sheets:** thin and flexible for cutting and embellishing
- **Upholstery foam:** for making pillows and cushions
- **Foam core sheets:** for backing, framing, and matting

Tips and Techniques

Here are a few handy tips and techniques for manipulating and assembling craft foam to make it just the right shape, size, or texture for your chosen project. Review this section before getting started and you'll be sure to have an easy time creating whatever you envision!

Shaping and Texturizing

Both textured and smooth foam sheets can be cut with a craft knife or a utility knife. Textured foam can also be cut with a more kid-friendly plastic serrated knife. Any rough edges on either type of foam can be smoothed out with a heat tool, emery board, or fine-grit sandpaper. A heat tool works well to cut, carve, or distress thick sheets and large shapes. There are handheld heat tools (air blowing or hot metal), as well as tabletop hot wire cutters that you operate like a scroll saw. You must always work outside or in a well-ventilated area when using heat tools with craft foam.

You can also add texture to the surface of smooth foam with a variety of tools. Add the look of snakeskin with the quick pass of a heat gun—the heat plumps up the foam cells. Use a stylus to make a pattern of dents, or try pressing rubber stamps into the surface to lightly deboss it.

Sanding. You can smooth out rough edges of foam with fine-grit sandpaper.

Carving. Use a heat tool to cut, carve, or distress foam shapes and sheets.

Texturizing. Add a snakeskin texture with a heat tool (top), use a stylus to add dents (left), or use rubber stamps to deboss foam (right).

Drilling Holes

Holes can be "drilled" into or straight through craft foam balls and other shapes with a sharp, sturdy wooden skewer. Twist the skewer as you slowly push it into or out of the foam. Going slowly will help you keep the skewer straight, and twisting will make a smooth channel and help to prevent the foam from chipping around the entrance and/or exit hole. If you need a hole that is larger than ⅛" (0.3cm) in diameter, start by making a small hole with a skewer, and then enlarge it by slowly pushing something thicker, like a knitting needle or chopstick, through the hole.

Drilling a hole. Drill a hole into a craft foam ball or shape with a wooden skewer by using a twisting motion.

Enlarging a hole. Enlarge a small hole made with a skewer by using a thicker object such as a knitting needle or chopstick.

Chipped foam. Oops! If you don't twist the skewer as you drill holes in foam, you may get a chipped entrance or exit hole.

Painting

Smooth foam can be painted with virtually any type of paint, ink, or dye without any surface prep. Opaque paint colors will cover the surface nicely with just one coat, while semi-opaque or transparent colors will require 2–3 coats for the best results. Painting textured foam can be a bit more challenging because it's not as dense, so it absorbs more of the paint color beneath the surface. You can prep the rough surface first with a special foam medium to fill in more of the texture before coloring it with paint, ink, or dye. Also, be aware that some types of household spray paint contain chemicals that can melt craft foam, so look for spray paints that say "safe for craft foam" on the label.

Using a toothpick or skewer pushed into the foam as a handle makes painting much easier, especially when painting balls. I have found that a wide, round-bristle brush works the best to evenly distribute paint on either type of craft foam. Pouncing ink or paint onto the surface with a foam brush or a wedge cosmetic sponge, as well as dip-dyeing with food coloring or fabric dyes, are some other fun techniques to try. Keep some scrap pieces or blocks of craft foam handy while painting; you can poke skewered, painted shapes into them to hold the shapes while they dry.

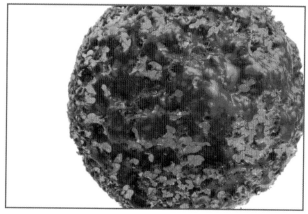

Melted spray-painted foam. Uh-oh! Be careful when painting foam; some household spray paints contain chemicals that melt it.

Toothpick handle. Paint craft foam shapes by skewering them with a toothpick and using that as a handle.

Pouncing. You can also paint craft foam by pouncing ink or paint onto the surface with a foam wedge.

Gluing

Liquid glues, tacky glues, and many dry adhesives work nicely on smooth foam. Thick tacky glues tend to work the best on textured foam, as they are not likely to sink down into open areas. Low-temperature hot glue guns also work well on both types of craft foam when you need quick-drying adhesion.

Tacky glue. Use thick, tacky glue on textured foam instead of thin, light glues. Thicker glues are less likely to sink into open areas.

Hot glue gun. A low-temperature hot glue gun is a quick-drying, easy way to glue foam pieces together.

Embellishing and Finishing

Toothpicks are indispensable for attaching two foam pieces together, and straight pins are the foam crafter's best friends for adding embellishments to foam quickly and easily. Both types of craft foam can be covered with glitter, fabrics, and fibers. Textured foam is particularly good for holding yarn and felt in place as you work without needing extra pins or adhesive. Smooth foam is an ideal surface for paper découpage techniques and creating fabric-covered panels.

Craft foam is so lightweight that a small loop of ribbon or floss glued to the back of a piece is strong enough for hanging. (You can also add straight pins for extra security.) Plus, the foam's light weight means you can use just a small straight pin or push pin in the wall when hanging your finished piece, leaving an almost imperceptible hole.

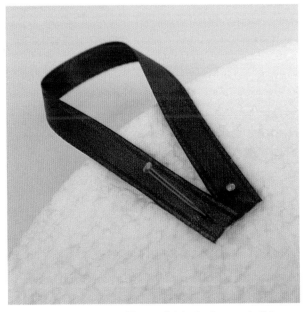

Loop for hanging. Glue a folded piece of ribbon to the foam and secure each end with a straight pin pushed into the foam at an angle to make a super simple and secure loop for hanging.

Materials

You probably already have many of the craft supplies used in this book on hand. I encourage you to think outside the box when you are looking for materials to embellish a foam foundation. Use your favorite colors and textures to make each project your own!

Fabric flowers

Beads

Seashells

Glitter

Spray paint

Baker's twine and other cording

Craft paint

Burlap

Felt

Washi tape

Fabric

Ribbon

Toothpicks

Cardstock

Chipboard letters

Straight pins (plain and decorative)

Dowels

Skewers

.7 m

Woodland Wreath

This sweet little tone-on-tone paper wreath will warmly welcome winter through your window. If you have a die-cutting machine or paper punches, you can cut all the leaves and circles quickly and easily.

Materials: Smooth foam wreath • Smooth or textured foam egg • Cardstock: two greens (4 sheets), brown (2 sheets), white • Standard ¼" (0.5cm) hole punch • Craft paint: green Craft glue • Toothpick • Straight pins • Ribbon

1 Cut 20 or more 2" (5cm) leaves each from two shades of green cardstock (by hand or with a punch/die). Cut 20 or more ¾" (2cm) circles from brown cardstock (by hand or with a punch/die). Punch 8–10 holes from white cardstock (using a standard hole punch).

2 To make the pinecone, layer and glue the bottom half of each brown circle to the egg, starting at the tip and working down to the base. Pin each circle at the bottom to secure it while the glue dries. Glue white dots on the front for snow.

3 Paint the foam wreath green and let it dry. Then pin the leaves to the front of the wreath in three overlapping rows, starting from the outside and working in toward the center, alternating the two shades of green.

4 Pierce the bottom of the pinecone with a toothpick and push the opposite end of the toothpick into the inside ring of the wreath. Attach a small ribbon loop to the back of the wreath for hanging.

Tip! Wrap a larger wreath with brown yarn to make this wreath even bigger. Just wrap the yarn tightly and secure the ends of the yarn to the back of the wreath with glue.

Washi Tape Décor Balls

Washi tape is easier to use than tissue paper for a torn paper collage effect, and you get the same randomly layered texture with the added bonus of super cute colors and patterns. Display a group of décor balls in a pretty bowl to add a pop of color to your coffee table.

Materials: Smooth foam balls • Washi tape: various patterns
Découpage medium • Toothpick

1 Pick one washi tape pattern per ball. Many tapes are semi-transparent, which allows the white surface of the ball to show through. Small prints like polka dots work best for a nice all-over pattern when you're finished.

2 Tear and press small strips of washi tape firmly against the ball, smoothing out any creases as you go. Position the pieces in random directions to get the nicest overall pattern.

3 Pierce the ball with a toothpick to use as a handle, and then coat the ball with a light layer of découpage medium. Poke the other end of the toothpick into a scrap piece of foam to hold the ball as it dries.

4 After the ball is dry, remove the toothpick and cover the hole with a small piece of washi tape. Then apply a little more découpage medium over the hole.

Entwined Wreath

Satin cord, paper cord, and baker's twine are great alternatives to yarn for wrapping balls and wreaths for a spring or summer look. The illusion of the balls floating almost in mid-air makes this particular wreath extra special. It looks great lying flat as part of a tablescape, too.

Materials: Smooth and textured foam balls • Textured foam wreath • Baker's twine, satin cord, paper cord, and other types of twine and cord • Clear gel craft glue Hot glue gun and glue sticks • Toothpicks

1 To wrap foam balls with any type of twine or cord, first tie a large knot at one end of the cord. Then make a hole in the ball and secure the knot inside it with glue. Place a pin in the hole so you can push the other end of the cord into it at the end.

2 To wrap smooth foam balls, add lines of clear gel glue to the ball while coiling and pressing the cord around the ball as shown. To wrap textured foam balls, wrap the ball tightly without glue, turning and twisting the ball as you wrap.

3 Wrap the wreath tightly with cord, securing the ends to the back with glue. Push a toothpick up through the wreath from the back where you want each ball to be placed, and then press a ball down on top of each toothpick.

4 Once you are happy with the arrangement, secure each ball to the wreath using a little hot glue at the base near the toothpick, as well as on the back of the wreath where the toothpick was inserted. Attach a loop for hanging at the top.

Tip! You can also create glitter balls (see page 28) or paint the balls before wrapping them to give your wreath some extra pops of color and sparkle.

Sandy Beach Sign

It's fun to paint and carve foam to look like the planks of a boardwalk! This summery beach sign isn't made of wood, though, so it can hang anywhere on just a small tack or push pin.

Materials: Smooth foam disc • Craft paint: blue, white • Chipboard letters
Sand dollars • Foam carving heat tool • Sand • Craft glue • Découpage medium
Skewer • Ribbon • Straight pins

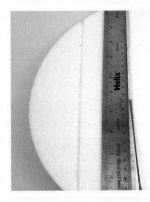

1 Carve evenly-spaced narrow channel lines into the foam disc with a heat tool (work outside or in a well-ventilated area), using a metal ruler as a guide. Use a skewer to clear away any melted foam residue from each channel.

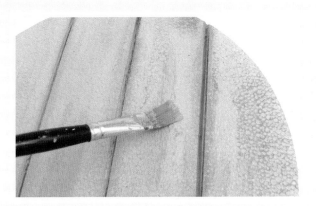

2 Paint the surface blue and let it dry.

3 Working in small sections, brush a generous coat of découpage medium onto the edge of the disc and press it into a pile of sand to coat the edge. Let it dry.

4 Paint the chipboard letters with white paint and let them dry. Glue the letters and sand dollars into position on the surface of the foam. Attach a ribbon loop on the back for hanging.

Triple-Take Mirrors

These cute little mirrors will dress up any space on your wall, reflect light and energy for better feng shui, or jazz up the inside of a school locker. Place them near your front door for that last-minute quick peek before inviting in guests who come knocking.

Materials: 3 smooth foam discs • 3 round mirrors • Craft paint • Craft glue
Heavy-duty craft glue • Ribbon • Straight pins

1 Paint the front and edges of each foam disc and let them dry.

2 Glue a ribbon around the edge of each disc and let the glue dry.

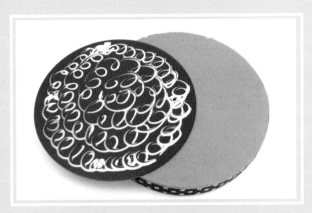

3 Use a generous amount of heavy-duty craft glue to adhere a mirror to the front of each painted disc and let the glue dry.

4 Attach a ribbon loop to the back of each disc for hanging separately. Arrange the mirrors in your preferred pattern on the wall.

Candy Stripes Wreath

Felt comes in so many fun, bright colors that it really is like buying candy when you shop for it! Make one of these wreaths for every family member in their favorite color combos to hang on their bedroom doors.

Materials: Textured foam wreath • Felt: multiple colors • Craft glue • Cardstock ring cut to match wreath • Large button • Large grommet • Grommet setting tool

1 Decide how to alternate the felt colors, and then cut the felt sheets into 1½" (4cm)-wide strips long enough to wrap around the wreath with some overlap at the back.

2 Wrap each strip of felt around the wreath. Overlap the strips at an angle (overlapping a little more on the inside edge than on the outer edge) to put the stripes on a slight diagonal. Glue all the strip ends to the back of the wreath.

3 Glue the cardstock ring to the back of the wreath. Wrap a wide, long piece of felt around the wreath to cover the final seam of the strips. Snip a hole through both layers of the felt hanger near the top and insert a grommet for hanging.

4 Cut some felt circles of varying sizes to layer under the button. Glue the circles and button onto the hanger strip of felt to accent it.

Country Cream Topiary

Flower topiaries are strikingly pretty, plus they're quick and easy to put together.
You can create several for party centerpieces in no time at all.

Materials: Textured foam ball • Smooth foam cube • Small square metal bucket
Wooden dowel • Fabric flowers: large cream burlap, small pink satin • Pearl-head
straight pins • Tacky glue • Pieces of cardstock, felt, and burlap • Skewer

1 Glue the foam cube to the bottom of the metal bucket, placing something heavy on top of the cube while the glue dries. If desired, paint the dowel pink and poke it into a scrap piece of foam to dry.

2 Arrange the large cream flowers openly and evenly around the ball and secure them with pearl-head pins. Fill the spaces with the small pink flowers.

3 Press one end of the dowel into the base of the ball, making a pilot hole with a skewer first. If desired, tie cream and pink ribbons into a bow around the dowel at the base of the ball and trim the ends as needed.

4 Cut a piece of cardstock and felt into squares large enough to cover the top of the bucket, plus a smaller piece of burlap. Slice a small X in the center of each square. Layer and glue on the foam cube as shown; insert the dowel through the X into the foam cube.

Crystal Snowball Garland

This dip-and-sprinkle technique is fun and kid-friendly—get the whole family involved in creating a long, sparkly holiday garland for your mantel, tree, staircase, or doorway.

Materials: Textured foam balls • Beading cord: blue • Découpage medium Glitter: blue, silver, gold • Crystal beads • Large upholstery needle • Skewers

1 Make a milky wash of découpage medium and water in a small bowl (about 1 part medium to 3 parts water). Skewer and dip each ball in the wash to coat them thoroughly. Tap each ball on the edge of the bowl to remove the excess wash.

2 Working over a paper plate or piece of paper or paper towel, sprinkle glitter generously all over each ball. Pour the excess glitter back into its container.

3 Poke the skewers of all the skewered balls into a scrap piece of foam to allow the balls to dry.

4 Once the balls are dry, remove the skewers and use the large needle to thread each ball onto the beading cord. Remove the needle to add the crystal beads where desired. Knot each end of the garland around a bead to secure it.

Romance Triptych Wall Panels

Show off your favorite fabrics with narrow wall panels, or even add appliqué to fabric for a real statement piece. The power of three is strong in the design world, but you can tile together as many panels as you like to make a beautiful statement on any wall.

Materials: 3 smooth foam panels • 3–4 coordinating fabrics • Fabric glue
Ball-head straight pins • Cardstock • Chipboard • Fusible tape • Ribbon

1 Cut three pieces of fabric to 3" (7.5cm) larger than the foam panels on all sides. Wrap each panel snugly, gluing the fabric edges to the back, mitering the corners like you would when wrapping a gift. Secure the fabric with pins until the glue is dry.

2 Choose a contrasting fabric to feature. Cut a chipboard sheet to the desired size for your focal panel. Trim the fabric to 1" (2.5cm) larger than the chipboard on all sides. Wrap the fabric around the chipboard and glue the edges to the back or iron fusible tape on low heat to the edges.

3 Pin the chipboard focal panel to one of the wrapped foam panels, placing the ball-head pins in each corner or all the way around the panel edges if desired.

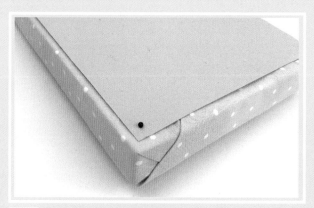

4 Trim sheets of cardstock to ½" (1.5cm) smaller than the foam panels on all sides, and glue them to the back of each foam panel to cover the fabric edges. Attach a ribbon loop to the back of each foam panel for hanging.

Pink Champagne
Party Garland

This bubbly garland will make everyone at the party want to cheer! Choose opaque paint colors for easy one-coat painting. Then stream the garland across the room, dribble it around a table, or let it drip down the backs of chairs.

Materials: Smooth foam balls: small, medium, large • Craft paint: pale pink, medium pink • Spray paint: gold metallic • Baker's twine: pink • 2 small beads Large upholstery needle • Skewers

1 Carefully push a skewer straight through the center of each ball to turn them into beads. Leave each ball on the skewer to use as a handle during painting. Paint each ball with 1 to 3 coats depending on the color opacity, varying the paint colors by ball size.

2 Poke the skewers into a scrap block of foam to let the balls dry between coats.

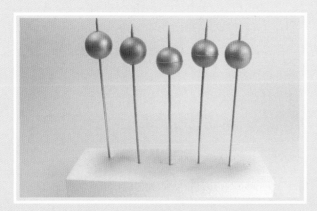

3 For the spray-painted balls, poke skewered balls into a scrap block of foam. Hold the block down and spray all the balls at once. Add a second coat after the first dries.

4 Remove all the skewers and use the large needle to thread the balls onto a long strand of baker's twine. Knot each end of the garland around a bead to secure it.

Beaded Burlap Tree

This decorative tree's neutral colors make it work all year long. Use a tight-weave burlap fabric and plenty of glue to minimize fraying as you work.

Materials: Textured foam cone • Burlap: gray • Pearl-head straight pins • Straight pins Round beads: white • Tacky glue • Hot glue gun and glue sticks

1 Cut a 2" (5cm)-wide strip of burlap that is long enough to wrap around the base of the cone. Glue it around the base of the cone, securing it with pins until the glue is dry.

2 Cut several strips of burlap about 2.5" x 4.5" (6.5 x 11.5cm). Working with one strip at a time, fold each in half lengthwise. Then glue the two short ends crossed over each other as shown with the folded edge facing up.

3 Glue and press each folded burlap "petal" onto the cone. Start at the bottom and secure each petal using two plain straight pins on each side and one pearl-head pin threaded through a bead in the center. Stagger the petals in each row.

4 Remove the plain pins once the glue has dried. To finish the tree, cut a circle of burlap and pin it to the top of the cone as shown (you may want to use glue or double-sided tape to get the folds to stay). Pin more beads to the top.

Tip! You can set your tree anywhere, as shown above, or you can glue it to a candle pedestal to really make it stand out, as shown on page 49. If the cone base is larger than the recessed area of the pedestal, first glue a circle cut from a sheet of foam core inside the pedestal, flush to the lip, to create a flat surface for adhering the cone.

Atomic Mobile

Put your own spin on planetary alignment—or shall we say DIY your DNA? This fun mobile makes a great decoration for kids' parties, or you can hang it in the nursery for the baby's visual delight.

Materials: Smooth foam balls: various sizes • Craft paint • Skewers • Paper cord • Craft glue • Heavy-duty scissors

1 Push a skewer into each ball and paint all the balls and skewers with 1 to 3 coats. The end of the skewer you hold while painting can stay unpainted, as it will be pushed into the center ball. Remove the skewer from the largest center ball.

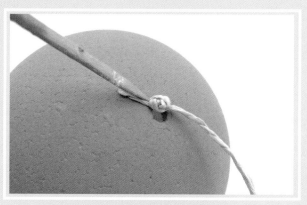

2 Tie a large knot at one end of a length of paper cord (you may need to make several knots on top of one another). Make a pilot hole in the largest ball, push the knot into the hole, and secure it with glue. Let it dry.

3 Push each skewered ball into the large ball so they orbit around it. Work with two balls at a time on opposite sides of the center ball so the mobile stays balanced. Trim the skewers to vary the distances. Secure each skewer with a little glue.

4 After sliding a drilled ball on to the string, tie a loop at the opposite end of the paper cord for hanging the mobile.

Mini Layer Cake

Make all your dinner guests feel extra special with a mini layer cake that has been baked and frosted just for them. Use the cakes as party favors or to customize each place setting.

Materials: Textured foam cylinders/discs • Scrapbook paper: various patterns • Foam carving heat tool • Tacky glue • Pearl-head straight pins • Mini faux flowers

1 Cut two cake layers of different diameters from the foam cylinders/discs. If you can't find two different size cylinders, trim one size down to a smaller size with a heat tool (work outside or in a well-ventilated area).

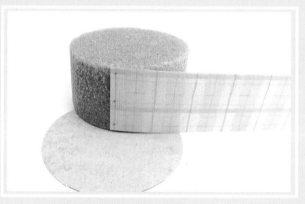

2 Cut a strip of scrapbook paper to match the height of each cake layer. Glue and wrap a strip around the edge of each layer, and pin the strips to secure them while they dry.

3 Cut circles of paper to the same diameter as each cake layer, and glue the circles to the top of each layer. Then glue the two layers together.

4 Push pearl-head pins into the foam to decorate the edges of the cake layers, and glue mini faux flowers to the top of each layer.

Scented Pearl Pomanders

With its relaxing scent, lavender is perfect for pomanders—but you can use any color and fragrance you like! Place one in a drawer, hang one in the closet, or display a bowl of them in the bathroom. They're also a lovely way to show off your most beautiful ribbons.

Materials: Textured foam balls • Lavender soap fragrance or essential oil (or scent of choice) Acrylic ink • Spray mister bottle • Pearl-head straight pins • Ribbon • Skewer

1 Blend several drops of ink and fragrance with about ½ cup of water in a spray bottle. Spray on a sheet of white paper to test the color, and add more fragrance or ink as needed.

2 Pour the ink mixture into a dish, push a skewer into a ball and dip the ball into the ink to coat thoroughly. Add a few more drops of fragrance directly on the top of the ball for a stronger scent if desired.

3 Once the ball is dry, wrap a ribbon around it (north and south), twist the ribbon at the base of the ball, and secure with a pin. Then wrap it back up to the top (east and west) and tie a bow.

4 Push pearl-head pins into the ball between the ribbons to further embellish it. Shorten the pins with wire cutters if necessary for small balls.

Modern Monogram Wall Panels

Because craft foam is so lightweight, it's the perfect surface for wall art that doesn't damage the walls. Fabric-covered panels are especially nice above the sofa or bed, and everyone loves a good excuse to display their favorite initial!

Materials: 4 smooth foam panels • 4 coordinating fabrics • Straight pins • Tacky glue Chipboard or craft foam letter • Ribbon

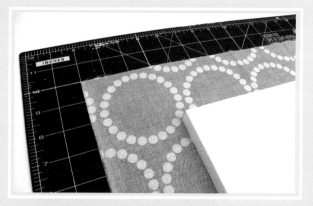

1 Press and then cut each fabric piece to 3" (7.5cm) larger than the foam panels on all sides.

2 Wrap each panel snugly with a piece of fabric, mitering the corners like you would when wrapping a gift box. Pin the edges of the fabric to the back of the panel, pushing the pins in at a slight angle.

3 Glue the letter to one panel and place a book on top while it dries.

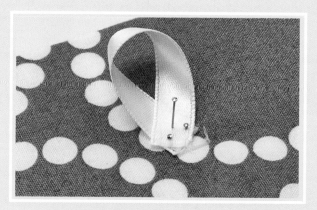

4 Attach a ribbon loop to the back of each panel for hanging. See the Romance Triptych Wall Panels on page 30 for directions on covering the fabric edges with a paper backer if desired.

Cake Pop Cube

Cake pops and lollipops are a whole lot sweeter when they're beautifully displayed. Make several cubes for the most pop-ular table at the party!

Materials: Large smooth foam cube • Patterned cardstock • Clear acetate sheet • Tacky glue Ribbon • Straight pins • Pearl-head straight pins • Hole punch • Skewer

1 Measure and cut 5 pieces of cardstock and a piece of clear acetate to fit the sides and top of the cube. You can leave the bottom uncovered, or you can cut a sixth piece of cardstock to cover it.

2 Spread a thin, even coat of glue over each side of the cube with a brush, going all the way out to the edges. Press cardstock onto each side of the cube and weight it with a book until dry.

3 Trim the top and bottom edges of the cube with ribbon secured with straight pins. Push the pins in at a slight angle down or up toward the center of the cube.

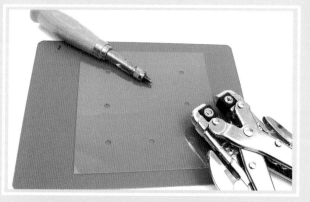

4 Punch a grid of holes in the center of the acetate and also in each corner. Secure the acetate to the cube with a pearl-head pin pushed in at an angle in each corner. Poke holes with a skewer through the acetate and cardstock into the foam.

Tip! Don't skip the acetate! It will help hold the cake pops secure and keep the paper from tearing.

Blooming Block

Narrow enough to sit on a windowsill, bookshelf, or the tiniest end table, this color-blocked block of blooms will brighten up any room with fresh or faux stems. It's an easy DIY centerpiece for a party table, too!

Materials: Smooth foam block • Floral water picks • Skewer • Craft paint • Painter's tape
Ribbon • Straight pins

1 Push each water pick straight down halfway into the top of the block and then remove them. Pick the loose foam bits out of the holes with a skewer, and then push each pick farther down into its hole, leaving the necks exposed.

2 Mask off a section around the entire block with painter's tape. Paint one color above the tape, including on the top of the block, and another color below. Carefully remove the tape and let the block dry.

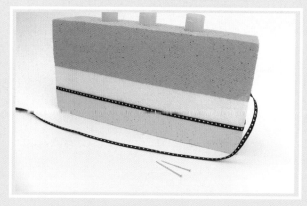

3 Trim the top and bottom of the unpainted area with ribbon, securing it with pins pushed into the foam.

4 Tie ribbon around the neck of each water pick. If desired, glue a couple of metal washers to the bottom of the block to weight it for stability, especially when filled with water and live blooms.

About the Author

Lisa Fulmer is an avid artist, a chronic crafter, and a devoted DIYer. As a professional designer and blogger for the craft industry, she gets to swim in paints, glitters, and glues on a daily basis, developing new project ideas and writing tutorials for a wide variety of craft websites, magazines, and manufacturers. In her role as the blog manager for the family-owned Plasteel Corporation (makers of Smoothfoam™), she works with a team of talented designers to bring crafters exciting new ideas for creating with craft foam every week.

Lisa's first book is *Craft Your Stash,* where she explores new ways to make creative gifts and home décor by digging into that big stash of craft supplies found in every crafter's closet. Check out more of her work at *LisaLizaLou.com.*

Acknowledgements

My sincerest gratitude goes to Julie and Bill for introducing me to the joys of creating with craft foam—and I gotta give a big "yo foamie!" shout-out to Julie for being such a supportive friend and colleague during these past few years.

Many thanks to all the designers on my craft foam team for their countless creative ideas—you all inspire me so much!

I would also like to express my deepest appreciation for everyone at Fox Chapel Publishing. The whole team is so helpful and wonderful to work with—editorial, design, photography, marketing, sales, and customer service—thank you all so much!

Acquisition editor: **Peg Couch**
Copy editor: **Katie Weeber**
Cover and layout designer: **Ashley Millhouse**
Editor: **Colleen Dorsey**
Project photography: **Scott Kriner**
Step-by-step photography: **Lisa Fulmer**